PIANO TIME PIECES

Book 1

27 companion pieces to Piano Time 1

new edition

T0057015

Pauline Hall

MUSIC DEPARTMENT

OXFORD
UNIVERSITY PRESS

OXFORD
UNIVERSITY PRESS

Great Clarendon Street, Oxford OX2 6DP, England
198 Madison Avenue, New York, NY10016, USA

Oxford University Press is a department of the University of Oxford.
It furthers the University's aim of excellence in research, scholarship,
and education by publishing worldwide

Oxford is a registered trade mark of Oxford University Press
in the UK and in certain other countries

© Oxford University Press 1989; new edition 2004

Pauline Hall has asserted her right under the Copyright, Designs
and Patents Act, 1988, to be identified as the Author of this Work

Database right Oxford University Press (maker)

This edition first published 2004

All rights reserved. No part of this publication may be reproduced,
stored in a retrieval system, or transmitted, in any form or by any means,
without the prior permission in writing of Oxford University Press,
or as expressly permitted by law. Enquiries concerning reproduction
outside the scope of the above should be sent to the Music Copyright
Department, Oxford University Press, at the address above

Permission to perform the works in this anthology in public
(except in the course of divine worship) should normally be obtained
from the Performing Right Society Ltd. (PRS), 29/33 Berners Street,
London W1T 3AB, or its affiliated Societies in each country throughout
the world, unless the owner or the occupier of the premises
being used holds a licence from the Society

Permission to make a recording must be obtained in advance
from the Mechanical Copyright Protection Society Ltd. (MCPS),
Elgar House, 41 Streatham High Road, London SW16 1ER,
or its affiliated Societies in each country throughout the world

ISBN 978-0-19-372785-4

Music and text origination by
Barnes Music Engraving Ltd., East Sussex
Printed in Great Britain on acid-free paper by
Halstan & Co. Ltd., Amersham, Bucks.

Copyright acknowledgement

Morning has broken (p. 5): text by Eleanor Farjeon. Reproduced by permission of
David Higham Associates Ltd, 5–8 Lower John Street, London, W1F 9HA.

Contents

Trick mirrors	4
Spooks	4
Morning has broken	5
Grass so green	6
Frog count	6
Allegretto	7
Bohemian dance	7
Martians' march	8
In the desert	9
A chat between friends	10
Turpin	10
The polar bear	11
On the river	12
See what I told you—so there!	12
Chinese take-away	13
Brave knight	14
Cheerful cha-cha-cha	15
Scarborough Fair	16
Easy going	17
Polly wolly doodle	18
The secret garden	19
Michael, row the boat ashore	20
Crocodile waltz	21
Song of the squeaky door	21
The witch's lair	22
Introduction and Promenade	23
Time to celebrate!	24

Trick mirrors

David Blackwell

Lively

Spooks

Pauline Hall

Mysteriously

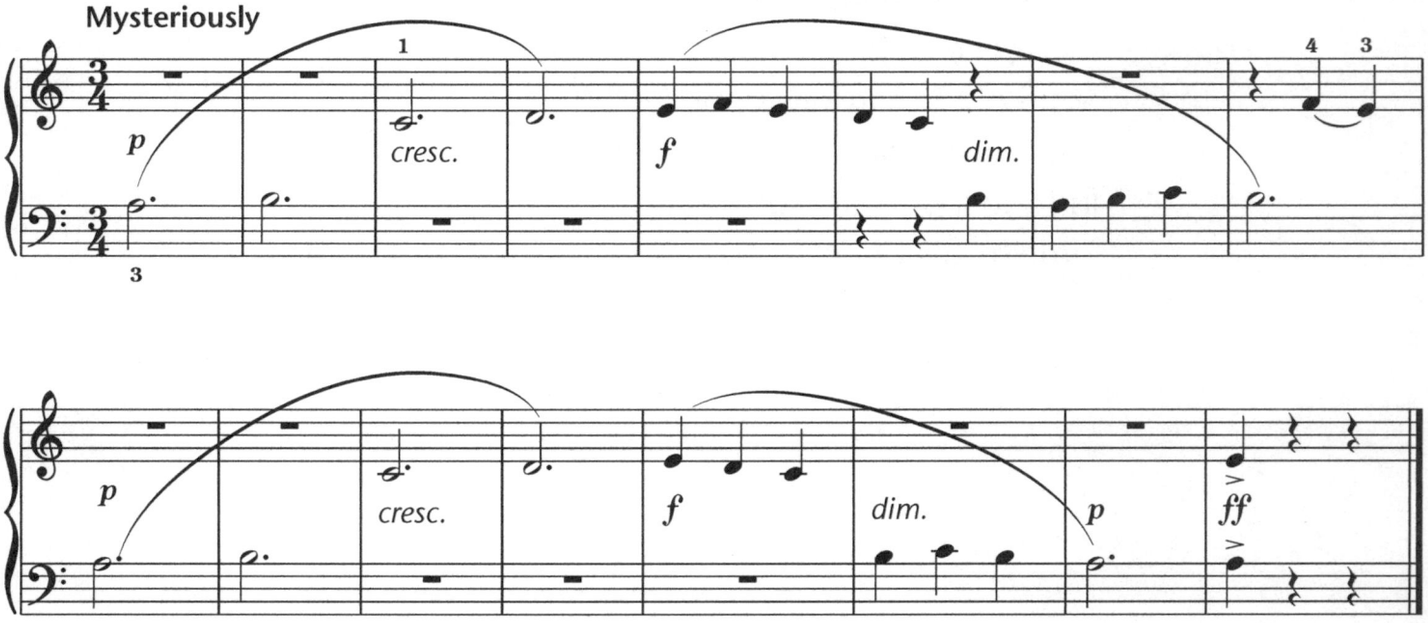

Morning has broken

Old Gaelic melody
Words by Eleanor Farjeon

Flowing
mf

Morn - ing has bro - ken like the first morn - ing;

Black - bird has spo - ken like the first bird.

Praise for the sing - ing! Praise for the morn - ing!

Praise for them spring - ing, fresh from the Word!

Text reprinted by permission of David Higham Associates Ltd.

Grass so green

Czech folk-tune
arr. Pauline Hall

Very smoothly

p legato

mp

p

Frog count

Pauline Hall

mf

Frogs are jump - ing in the sun, Can you count them one by one?

Nine - teen frogs and one frog more Make just twen - ty, that's a score!

Allegretto

Daniel Gottlob Türk
(1756–1813)

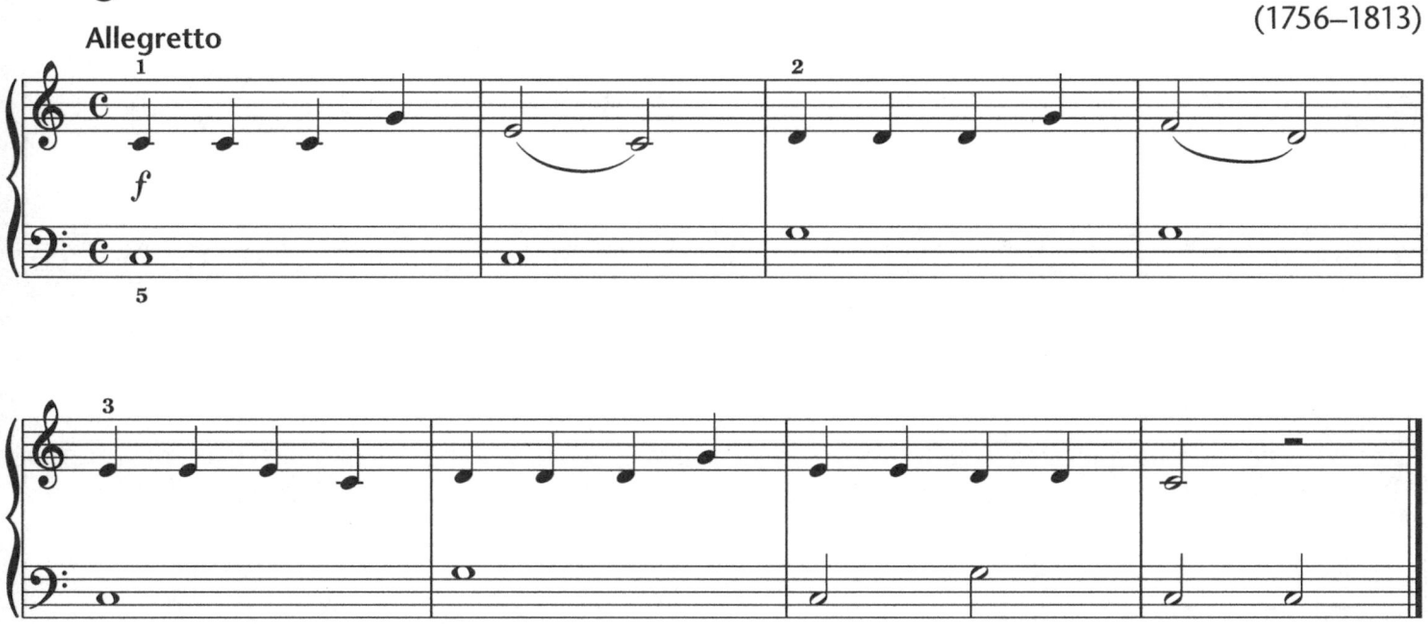

Bohemian dance

Czech folk-tune
arr. Pauline Hall

Martians' march

Pauline Hall

Crash land onto a group of low notes as loudly as possible!

In the desert

Pauline Hall

Steadily

A chat between friends

Alan Bullard

Turpin

Pauline Hall

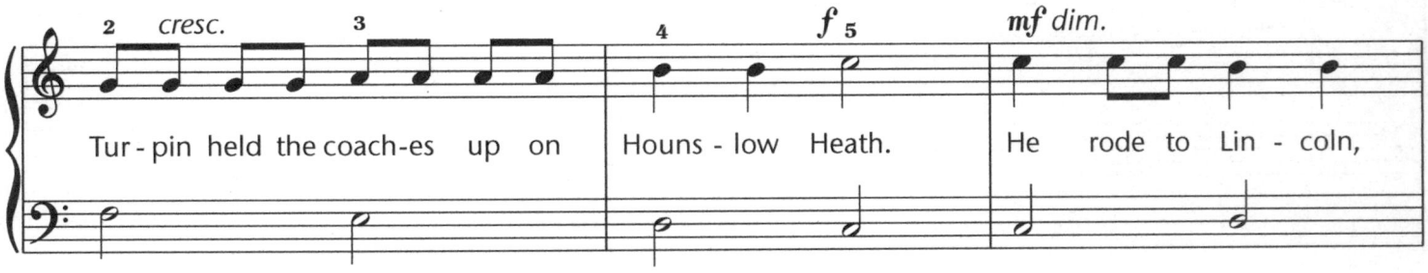

The polar bear

Melody 19th century
arr. Pauline Hall

mf

We sing of the po - lar bear, fear - less and bold; He

ne - ver feels hot and he ne - ver feels cold, Be -

- cause where he lives sum - mer ne - ver oc - curs, And the

rest of the year he wears plen - ty of furs.

On the river

Alan Bullard

Flowing

See what I told you—so there!

Pauline Hall

Lively

Chinese take-away

Here's a chance to invent your own tune!
Play steady F♯ and C♯ crotchets in the left hand. In the right hand, follow the rhythm given and make up a tune using the black keys only. The last note should be an F♯.

Steadily

Brave knight

Moritz Vogel
(1846–1922)

Like a march

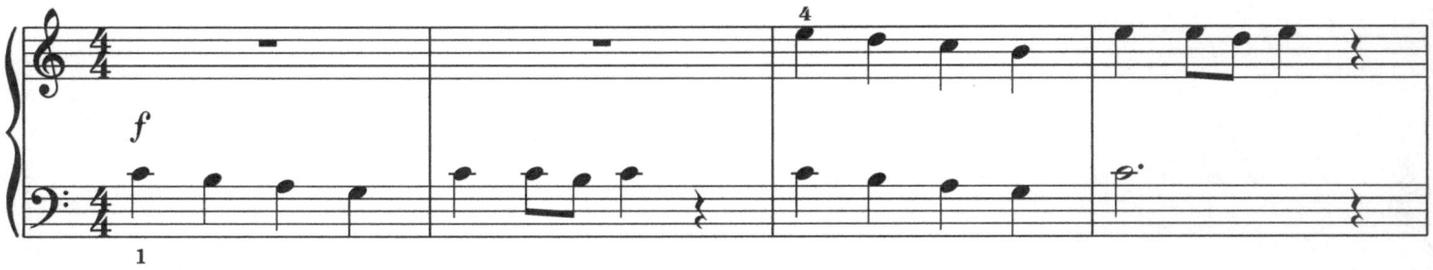

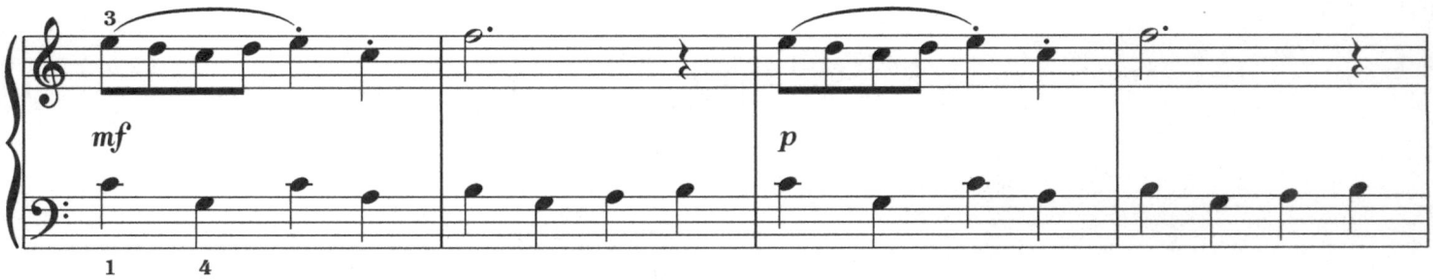

Cheerful cha-cha-cha

Pauline Hall

Scarborough Fair

English folk-tune

Easy going

David Blackwell

Cheerfully

mf

f

Polly wolly doodle

American traditional

Cheerfully

mf

f

The secret garden

Pauline Hall

You can use the sustaining (right) pedal to give a more mysterious effect. Put the pedal down at the beginning of each two-bar phrase, and lift it up on the last crotchet.

Slowly and mysteriously

p

p

p

p

p

rit.

pp

Michael, row the boat ashore

American folk-tune

On the move

mf

f

slower

mp

p

Crocodile waltz

Alan Bullard

Song of the squeaky door

Alan Bullard

The witch's lair

Pauline Hall

Two pieces:

Alexander Reinagle
(1756–1809)

1. Introduction

Allegretto

2. Promenade

Andante

Time to celebrate!

Alan Bullard

Rhythmically

f

mf

f

p

mf

f

ff